When Sammy Met Sunny

Written by Hannah Maloney
& Illustrated by Kylene Marie

For all children to learn how to stay safe around dogs.

For all families and educators to encourage responsible pet ownership, and to create a safe and harmonious co-existence between people, pets and places.

Sunshine Coast Council

Sunshinecoast.qld.gov.au

First published in Australia

© Sunshine Coast Council 2022

Illustrated by Kylene Marie

Sunshine Coast Council

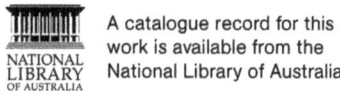
A catalogue record for this work is available from the National Library of Australia

ISBN: 978-0-6455000-0-4

This book is copyright. The right of Sunshine Coast Council to be identified as the author of this book has been asserted by them in accordance with the Copyright Act 1968.

Apart from any use as permitted under the Act, no part may be reproduced, copied, scanned, stored in a retrieval system, recorded or transmitted, in any form or by any means, nor may or any other exclusive right be exercised, without the prior written permission of the copyright owner.

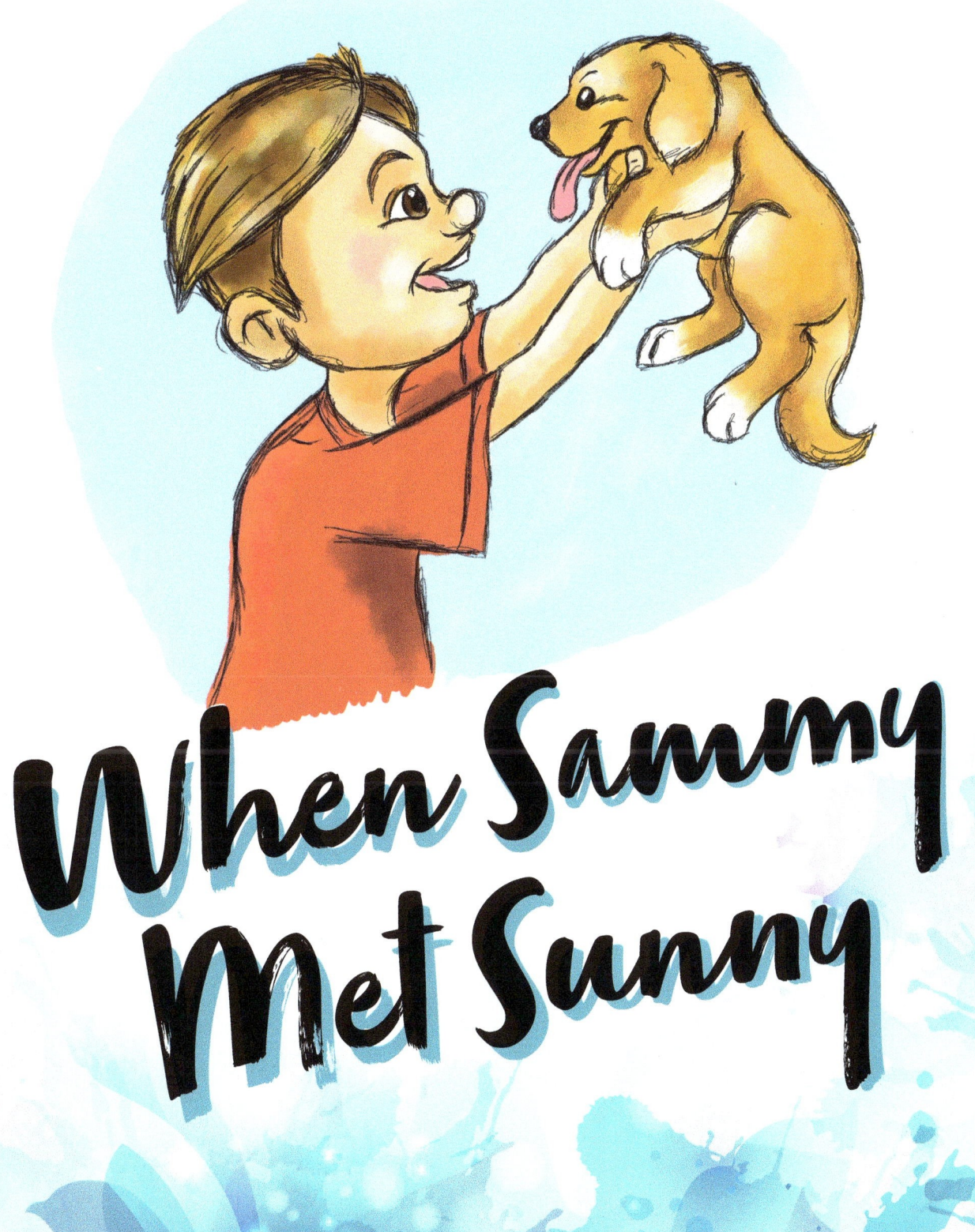

Sammy always wanted a dog.

A warm, furry, friendly dog.

A PART OF HIS FAMILY.

Marli was Sammy's best friend at school, and she had a dog named Willow.

Willow recently had puppies, so Sammy and his parents visited Marli's house.

THE PUPPIES WERE SO CUTE!

Some were black and some were brown.
Some were thin and some were round.
But they all made tiny, whimpering sounds.

'I LIKE THIS ONE,' Sammy said. 'CAN I KEEP HIM?'

'A dog is a BIG responsibility,' Sammy's dad said.

'They need walks and healthy food to eat.'

MY PARENTS SAY THERE
ARE RULES WITH A PET

KEEP THEM FED
AND VISIT THE VET

THERE'S ALSO RULES
TO KEEP KIDS SAFE

AS DOGS CAN BITE
AND THAT'S NOT OKAY.

That night, Sammy told his mum how he would play fetch with the dog, take it for walks and care for it.

'You still need to learn how to be SAFE around dogs,' she said.

'But I learnt all about staying safe around dogs at school,' Sammy said.

'I'll prove to you that I am responsible, and that I am safe. In fact, I am SUPER SAFE!'

The next day, Sammy was shopping with his mum at the local markets, when something caught his eye.

IT WAS A DOG, TIED UP AND ALL ALONE.

'Hello, doggy. What's your....

Ah ha!' said Sammy.
'My first super safety tip!'

SAMMY'S SUPER SAFETY LIST!

LEAVE A LITTER OF PUPPIES ALONE!

DON'T HUG DOGS TOO CLOSELY

NEVER REACH IN A CAR DOOR TO PAT A DOG!

LEAVE DOGS ALONE WHEN THEY ARE SLEEPING!

NEVER PAT A DOG THAT IS ALONE! ☑

NEVER PAT A DOG WHEN THEY ARE EATING!

STAND TALL LIKE A TREE, DON'T SCREAM, RUN OR HIDE!

NEVER PAT AN INJURED OR SICK DOG

BE QUIET AND CALM AROUND DOGS

IF A DOG IS TIED UP IN
THE DISTANCE

ASK THE OWNER FOR
SOME ASSISTANCE

NEVER TOUCH A DOG THAT
IS ALL ALONE

OR GRAB A DOG THAT'S
OUT TO ROAM.

Sammy and mum then went to visit Marli's house again.

'Hi, Marli,' Sammy said. 'How is Willow today?'

WILLOW WAS ENJOYING HER DINNER SO MUCH SHE HAD NO IDEA SAMMY WAS EVEN THERE.

Sammy stepped back. 'Ah ha!' he whispered to himself, 'another super safety tip.'

SAMMY'S SUPER SAFETY LIST!

- LEAVE A LITTER OF PUPPIES ALONE!
- DON'T HUG DOGS TOO CLOSELY
- NEVER REACH IN A CAR DOOR TO PAT A DOG!
- LEAVE DOGS ALONE WHEN THEY ARE SLEEPING!
- NEVER PAT A DOG THAT IS ALONE! ☑
- NEVER PAT A DOG WHEN THEY ARE EATING! ☑
- STAND TALL LIKE A TREE, DON'T SCREAM, RUN OR HIDE!
- NEVER PAT AN INJURED OR SICK DOG
- BE QUIET AND CALM AROUND DOGS

AN IMPORTANT TIME TO
LEAVE DOGS ALONE

IS WHEN THEY'RE EATING
DINNER OR A BONE

NEVER TOUCH THEIR FOOD,
BOWL OR HEAD

OR LAY DOWN TO PLAY IN
THEIR FLUFFY DOG BED.

'See you at school,' Marli called to Sammy.

'Bye Marli, bye Willow,' Sammy said as he skipped through the front gate. 'I'm off to soccer now.'

When Sammy arrived at soccer, he quickly got changed and ran onto the field.

He was so excited to play that he almost didn't see the large dog running towards him.

SAMMY WAS SO SCARED THAT HIS LEGS FELT LIKE JELLY.

But then he remembered the safety lesson at school. So he took a deep breath and thought, 'Ah ha! I know exactly what to do with this super safety tip.'

SAMMY'S SUPER SAFETY LIST!

LEAVE A LITTER OF PUPPIES ALONE!
DON'T HUG DOGS TOO CLOSELY
NEVER REACH IN A CAR DOOR TO PAT A DOG!
LEAVE DOGS ALONE WHEN THEY ARE SLEEPING!
NEVER PAT A DOG THAT IS ALONE!
NEVER PAT A DOG WHEN THEY ARE EATING!
STAND TALL LIKE A TREE, DON'T SCREAM, RUN OR HIDE!
NEVER PAT AN INJURED OR SICK DOG
BE QUIET AND CALM AROUND DOGS

IF A STRANGE DOG COMES
CHARGING UP TO YOUR SIDE

STAND TALL LIKE A TREE,
DON'T SCREAM, RUN OR HIDE

KEEP YOUR ARMS TUCKED IN,
TAKE THREE STEPS BACK

THIS WILL KEEP YOU SAFE
FROM AN ATTACK.

After soccer, Sammy read over his checklist of how to stay safe around dogs.

Arriving home, Sammy called out, 'Dad! Dad! I told you I would prove that I am responsible, and that I am safe. In fact, I am SUPER SAFE!'

'Well,' his dad said, 'you will have to show me your checklist.' But Sammy suddenly felt nervous. He wondered whether the checklist was enough to show how safe he can be around dogs.

'I love dogs so so much,' cried Sammy, 'but I also know I need to give them space, and leave them alone when they are sleeping, and play calmly around them, and...'

His dad smiled. 'We are so proud of you, Sammy. You have shown us you can be safe AND responsible around dogs. So... there is a surprise for you in your bedroom.'

'Really?' Sammy said, then he ran to his bedroom door where he heard a tiny whimper.

Sammy grinned, took a deep breath, then opened the door...

For more information about dog safety tips please visit Council's website

Sunshinecoast.qld.gov.au

www.ingramcontent.com/pod-product-compliance
Lightning Source LLC
Chambersburg PA
CBHW061139010526
44107CB00069B/2989